Praise for *Remedy for Burnout: 7 Prescriptions Doctors Use to Find Me...*

The practice of medicine is ... professions humans have ever ... most demanding. The professi... ...proving to be actually destructive to many physicians, as the essence of healing has become progressively eliminated through insanities too numerous to name. For many physicians, the magical intimacy of the doctor-patient relationship is little more than a distant memory. For all this, however, there is a way out. In this eminently hopeful, personal, down-to-earth book, Dr. Starla Fitch shares what has worked for her. This is a report from the front, from a medical insider who's been in the trenches and knows how to speak from her heart. *Remedy for Burnout: 7 Prescriptions Doctors Use to Find Meaning in Medicine* is really a hero's journey—a report from one who has braved challenging experiences and returns to share lessons learned. I cannot imagine a physician who would not benefit from this book. I heartily recommend it to patients as well, because it is an opportunity for them to peek behind the curtain. I know my fellow physicians will share my enthusiastic response to this fine book: recalling why we entered medicine to begin with, why it once enchanted us, and how it can again. Thank you, Dr. Starla, for this great gift.

**—Larry Dossey, MD, author of *Healing Words: The Power of Prayer and the Practice of Medicine* and *One Mind: How Our Individual Mind Is Part of a Greater Consciousness and Why It Matters***

If you are a doctor or any health-care practitioner who needs some rekindling of your original passion to help people, this is the book for you. Starla Fitch's purpose to help health-care professionals move from burnout to vitality comes through loud and clear in this book. I highly recommend it.

**—Steve Sisgold, author of *What's Your Body Telling You?***

Deep in the heart of every physician is the desire to help a fellow human being—to alleviate suffering—and a love for the art of practicing medicine. Unfortunately, in the present world of medicine, the sacred connection to our heart's desire to be healers is challenged and overwhelmed by external pressures. In a broken medical system, the physician is too often vilified for problems that feel out of our control. A tipping point has been reached where myriad external demands such as administrative duties, medical-school debt, and overbooked clinics are leading to burnout in our careers. Career burnout is prevalent in our society yet not openly addressed in the medical field. There is an unspoken code in our rigorous medical training of "toughing it out." Record numbers of physicians report symptoms of burnout but when one is suffering, it is all too common to feel isolated and at a loss for where to turn for help. Dr. Starla Fitch's book offers a heart-centered remedy on how physicians can heal themselves, feel empowered, reconnect to their life purpose, and truly learn how to love medicine despite the challenges of the external world.

**—Romila "Dr. Romie" Mushtaq, MD, neurologist specializing in mind-body medicine, speaker, writer, and national mindful living expert**

# REMEDY FOR BURNOUT

# REMEDY FOR BURNOUT

*7 Prescriptions Doctors Use*
*to Find Meaning in Medicine*

Starla Fitch, MD

LANGDON STREET PRESS

Langdon Street Press
322 First Avenue N, 5th floor
Minneapolis, MN 55401
612.455.2293
www.langdonstreetpress.com

ISBN-13: 978-1-63413-027-1
LCCN: 2014948353

Distributed by Itasca Books

Edited by: Glad Doggett and Beth Kujawski
Cover design: Andy Carpenter Design
Interior design: Sabrina Landers
*Printed in the United States of America*

# CONTENTS

# ACKNOWLEDGMENTS

Having never birthed a baby, I can only imagine what mothers go through for nine months. With birthing this book, the gestation period was a long twenty-three months, and there was no epidural available for the delivery. Luckily, I had a team of "midwives" along the way who helped me in this process.

"Thanks" always seems like such a small word at times like this. And there will likely be people who are inadvertently left out of this list. My gratitude extends so far and wide that I could probably write another book on that alone.

To my editor, Glad Doggett, who kept me sane while humoring me to tackle a section just one more time, who cheered me on when my lizard brain reared its ugly head, who worked nights and weekends when my creativity was in overdrive: you are the best.

To my format and word specialist, Beth Kujawski, who stepped up and worked her magic to put the final polish on this project: thank you! Your faithful support, humor, and wisdom saw me through revisions too numerous to count. I am grateful for you.

To Andy Carpenter, the best book cover genius ever, who took an idea and found the perfect vision: thank you.

To my graphic designer, Sabrina Landers, who was able to translate my thoughts into beautiful designs that spoke to my heart and to my visions for my work here and on my website: you are amazing.

To my virtual assistant, Susan Lucibello, and my computer wizard, Stacey Pruim, who have managed to get my website and my message out into the world despite my major deficit of technical knowledge: deep thanks and gratitude for bearing with me and keeping me on track and online.

To my business coaches and mentors for the past few years: Lissa Rankin, MD, Dr. Martha Beck, Christine Kane, Michele Woodward and Lisa Zimmerman. Each of you has added so much to the person I am today. You have each taken a part of me that needed expansion and showed me how to expand in ways that are authentic to my purpose.

To all the physicians who were gracious enough to participate in the interviews, many of which ran over an hour, and who not only gave me their time and energy, but showed me how vulnerability can lead to greatness: thank you from the bottom of my heart for helping me to remember why I went into medicine in the first place. Without each of you, this book would not have been possible.

For my colleagues, operating room staff, and office staff, especially my assistant, Indira Shockley: thank you for allowing me the time I needed to pursue this passion so that we may help others in medicine who are struggling.

For my patients, who remind me daily of why I am one of the luckiest people on the planet to be able to serve you with love and respect, and who remind me every day that it is *you* who help me in the process, not the other way around.

For my friends and family, who were always there,

## Acknowledgments

whether my ideas seemed good or lame, and who built me up and kept me moving forward, especially Jen, Aurelia, Sherri, Eric and my Sisterhood of Doctors. You all deserve a medal for the past several months! Thank you.

And thank you to the true love of my life: my husband, Chris. You are my support, my guide, my muse, and my sounding board. Thank you for listening, whether you really wanted to or not. For offering an opinion when you had had a long day of surgery. For encouraging me in your gentle, loving way by not asking for anything but my love over the past several months. "It's all for you," as the song says.

I love ewe.

# FOREWORD

The problem for doctors is that they receive information but not a true education. I felt this pain when I started practicing medicine and wrote to the dean of my medical school about what I felt was needed in medical education and training. He never answered my letter. It took fifty years, and several mailings of my letter, to get an answer from a new dean.

Through my years practicing medicine, I've learned to treat people, not just their diseases. The rewards from this lesson were sweet but hard earned. For example, one patient asked me to escort her down the aisle on her wedding day. Yet, years before, when I treated her for severe burns, she had screamed "I hate you" to me in the hospital due to the pain caused by the treatment.

Another patient shifted the course of my life when he said, "You're a nice guy, and I feel better when I am in the office with you. But I can't take you home with me. So I need to know how to live between office visits."

I started group therapy to help my patients live between visits and discovered that when you help them live, they also live longer, healthier lives. In a sense, I became a loving father figure for them.

But that kind of connection exacts a toll. And in our day-to-day lives, what we do not express ultimately presents its bill through its effect upon our minds and bodies. If doctors were more willing to look within, they would find happiness.

Dr. Starla understands this truth because she was once one of the doctors who struggled to find a balance between her life and practice. The demands of the medical profession are profound and vast: life-and-death decisions, rigorous— if not grueling—schedules, and bureaucracy that knows no bounds. It makes many doctors weary.

But Starla believes that doctors can learn to love medicine again. And she has dedicated herself to showing others the way to the balance she desperately sought— and found. Through lovemedicineagain.com and now this book, she shares her warmth and wisdom with us and invites us to rediscover the healthy and unhealthy reasons we entered the field and that the ultimate solution is to be found in caring for people and not just treating their diseases.

—Bernie Siegel, MD, author of *Love, Medicine & Miracles*
and *The Art of Healing*

# PART I

## DIAGNOSING
## THE PROBLEM

# CHAPTER 1

# START WHERE
# YOU ARE

The author, teacher, and pioneer in integrative medicine, Dr. Rachel Naomi Remen, says, "Although we work in a system that's broken, our work is not broken."[1]

I would add to Rachel's insight: however, *we* may be a bit broken.

You can hardly pick up a newspaper or magazine these days without reading one more take on the new health-care system and its impact on medicine. That focus is almost always about how patients will fare in this brave new world. That makes sense when one considers that, at some point, we all are likely to be patients.

But the question many of us have is this: How will changes to health care really affect physicians?

My intention is not to hammer out policy or procedure. That is neither my forte nor my interest. I will leave that discussion to those people who relish ironing out decades-old difficulties created by more than one group of people.

No, my focus is on helping those of us on the front lines. Here and now.

Most of us followed a calling to serve others through practicing medicine. We spent years garnering knowledge through medical school, internship, and residency—even fellowship. We have dedicated our time, talent, and treasure to healing others.

But as we learned to heal others, many of us forgot how to heal ourselves.

The level of burnout among physicians is at an all-time high. Many people outside our profession (and even some within it) feel the dissatisfaction stems from changing economics. While certainly this adds fuel to the fire of discontent, I think a great many of my burned-out colleagues are frustrated with the changes in the relationships within medicine. One such dysfunctional relationship is the tie between doctors and insurance companies.

Here's a case in point: A large managed-care network recently removed my practice from its list of preferred providers.

Had we not taken good care of our patients? Weren't we available for those patients 24/7? Did patients complain that my partners and I did not deliver quality care?

No. No. And no.

The managed-care network decided to provide the types of services we provide. It opted to move the services in-house to save money, regardless of the consequences to its patients.

How did this affect my patients and my practice? One affected patient was recently diagnosed with eyelid cancer. I scheduled her surgery to remove the growth, followed by another surgery for reconstruction. She was set to proceed when her network informed her she must find a new, in-network doctor to perform the procedures or be responsible for her bill.

Another of my patients had been seeing me regularly to monitor for recurrence. Two years before, I treated her for a rare type of eyelid cancer. With her particular diagnosis, the possibility for recurrence is high. She had opted for regular checkups every three months. She, too, was told by the insurance network to find a new physician for her continued care.

I believe the loss of continuity that has emerged in our health-care system has not only disrupted our patients' health, it has disrupted physicians' quality of care.

Discontinuity takes the "care" out of patient care.

What can doctors do?

Well, we can stamp our feet a couple times and shake our fists at the sky. We can even shed a few tears.

We can shout out, "Dammit, life is not always fair!"

But then we must choose to take action in our lives and in our practices.

That's what I mean when I say you need to start where you are.

Doctors still make a difference in people's lives. We can serve a higher good and love our work—maybe not all day, every day. I am not sure that's possible for anyone. But I am certain we can take positive steps toward believing in our calling again.

According to a survey in *Medical Economics*, more than one third of physicians who responded to the survey reported that if they could go back in time, they would choose a different specialty or a different career altogether.[2] A mere 41 percent of respondents said they would recommend medical practice to the younger generation.

In 2011, in an online questionnaire of twenty-four thousand doctors representing twenty-five specialties, only 54 percent said they would choose medicine again as a career, down from 69 percent in 2010. Only 41 percent said they would choose the same specialty again. Less than 25 percent said they would choose the same practice setting, compared with 50 percent the previous year.[3]

Physicians are burning out in record numbers. In an excellent article on KevinMD.com, anesthesiologist Dr. Karen Sibert discussed the difference between burnout and disillusionment.[4] One could argue that many of those dissatisfied doctors are "disillusioned." True burnout is clinically defined in the ICD-10 codes as a "state of vital exhaustion."

Stanford social psychologist Christina Maslach developed a quantitative tool more than thirty years ago to look at the problem of disillusionment. The Maslach Burnout Inventory reviews three factors: emotional exhaustion, depersonalization, and personal accomplishment.

Emotional exhaustion measures feelings of being emotionally overextended and exhausted by one's work. Depersonalization measures an unfeeling and impersonal response toward recipients of one's service, care, treatment, or instruction. And personal accomplishment measures feelings of competence and successful achievement in one's work.

When the Maslach scale was used to evaluate burnout among US physicians, nearly 38 percent cited high emotional exhaustion, 29 percent experienced high depersonalization, and 12 percent experienced a low sense of personal accomplishment.[5]

As one would suspect, different specialties had different degrees of burnout. In 2013, a large survey revealed that 50 percent of doctors in critical care, emergency medicine, and family medicine matched the burnout criteria. Doctors with specialization in OB/GYN experienced the highest level of burnout, with many anticipating leaving medicine altogether.[6]

More than four hundred physicians commit suicide in the US each year.[7] The suicide rate for female physicians is two and half to four times higher than the general population.

Houston, we have a problem.

When I set out on my road to medicine, I, too, had high hopes and a deep conviction for helping others.

Remembering *why* we got into medicine in the first place can often soften the edges of long, difficult days.

My story unfolded on a circuitous route to med school. I started with a master's degree in sociology, and my first job after I graduated was working for the Virginia Center on Aging.

I administered hour-long assessment surveys to the elderly population of the state. I would drive my old Volkswagen to the specified house on the survey map and cold call these older folks, asking if I could come into their homes to assess their needs.

In retrospect, I can see how much the world has changed. I would never consider doing such a thing these days. Back then, I didn't even have a cell phone to call for backup. In fact, the only time I wouldn't knock on the door was when there was an electric fence or a really mean-looking dog in the yard.

As I completed the surveys, I would hear the same answers over and over whenever I asked the older people about their medical problems. They would tell me they were taking a pink pill, but they weren't sure what it was for. When I asked why they didn't know the name of their medication or why they were taking it, they would tell me their doctors "didn't have time" to explain it to them.

Huh?

Back then, doctors had a bit more time in their offices to spend with patients.

Why, then, were doctors not taking the time to do something as simple as explain a new medication to a patient?

After hearing the same responses nearly fifty times in the first three months, I began to feel a nudge to do something better for these people and others like them.

I had always had part-time jobs in the medical field while I was in school: I worked as an EKG technician, as a ward clerk, and as a medical assistant.

After spending months working in the field with the survey respondents, I felt compelled to apply for medical school. I signed up for a semester of premed classes while I continued to work.

I called my parents one night to tell them about my decision. In my family, it was understood that I had to support myself during my schooling. My call was more of a request for emotional support than one of financial support. Nonetheless, I will never forget my dad's response: "That is the dumbest idea I have ever heard! I don't think you have any idea what you are talking about, and we do not support you in this. Period."

Wow.

So much for all those parents who are excited when their children decide to be doctors.

Well, long (very long!) story short, I did the premed work and was accepted into medical school, followed by my ophthalmology residency and then my oculoplastic fellowship.

At my medical school graduation, my dad wrote on the card: "Guess I was wrong."

In retrospect, I think his reaction served me well. It made me stronger and more determined to reach my goal. But after landing what I believed to be my perfect job in my perfect location, I realized that it wasn't all so perfect after all.

Patients didn't follow my medical advice. Insurance companies decided which surgeries I could and could not perform. (Imagine having to fight with an insurance company for approval to do a surgery on a twenty-year-old with a cancer diagnosis. I asked the company's representative, "What part of the word *cancer* don't you understand?") I had to work alongside partners with different expectations of how the business of medicine should be carried out. And my days were filled with more paperwork than patient work.

I spent several years pushing a boulder uphill, crying over silly songs on the radio during my drives home and constantly telling myself that surely it didn't have to be like this.

Then, one day, I realized I was right. My life, my practice, my way of working didn't have to be like that. There were things that I could do, things I had seen other doctors do, that worked.

And that's when my heart and my head began to work together to build a world where I could truly love medicine again.

What I've learned on this journey is that the cure to what ails us is different for each of us. Your remedy may not be my remedy. And that's okay. My goal is to show you different tactics and strategies that have worked for me and other doctors who have come to love medicine again.

Some doctors have questioned their priorities. Others have altered the way they practice medicine to realign with their true purpose. But the common thread that ties us together is that we have all come to know a renewed satisfaction in our daily work as healers.

That is what I want for you. And that is why I wrote this book.

# PART II

## PERSONAL
## PRESCRIPTIONS

# CHAPTER 2

# DEVELOP RESILIENCE

"If we don't allow ourselves to experience joy and love, we will definitely miss out on filling our reservoir with what we need when . . . hard things happen."
—Dr. Brené Brown

**R**esilience is tenacity.

It's the ability to bounce back and be strong or healthy after something bad happens.

How does resilience apply to being a physician? In just about every way. In every step of training that we take as doctors, we must bounce back.

Do you remember in medical school when the teachers used the Socratic Method to challenge your memory, and a good "dressing down" was part of the drill? When they asked you to recall the four causes of fever after surgery, did you get partial credit for naming only three? Yeah, me neither.

Do you remember those nights "on call" when you were awakened at 2:00 a.m. by the nurse and couldn't remember your name for a minute, let alone the normal levels for serum potassium? Did the nurse give you a break or did she repeat the lab values at a fast clip because she figured that she had been up all night, so you may as well be too?

For a brief moment (please, don't linger on this one!), think back to your board exams. And maybe even your renewal of your board exams. Just taking them, let alone passing them, should be in the dictionary when you look up the word "resilience."

After the rigors of medical school, internship, residency, fellowship, boards, and finding your first job as a "real" doctor were behind you, were your resilience tests finished?

If you're at all like me, the answer is a resounding "No way!" Maybe even a "Hell no!"

Every day in the office, we doctors must renew our ability to provide proper care for our patients.

On a normal day, resilience may look like the simple act of taking extra time to delicately tell a patient she has cancer then having to steel yourself for the next patient, who is angry because you are running twenty minutes behind schedule.

Or resilience may be required in the middle of your ten-minute lunch break while you endure a conference call with a patient's insurance company during which you explain why reconstructing tissue after removing a cancerous growth is not a cosmetic procedure.

Or maybe resilience is bouncing back after you say no to your child's teacher when she asks you to use your few hours of free time to bake cookies for the class. Again.

While resilience is helpful to many, it is crucial in the lives of physicians, who often face life-and-death situations with their patients.[1] Those of us who develop the practice of changing course in the face of changing demands are the ones who best meet such challenges head-on.[2]

Research shows that four personality traits are especially important in developing resilience: self-directedness, cooperativeness, harm avoidance, and persistence.[3]

In my interviews with doctors who rediscovered meaning in medicine, I found they all relied on resilience. In fact, the levels of persistence these men and women maintain are heroic.

When I talked with Dr. William Barber, a top breast cancer surgeon in Atlanta, Georgia, he shared an amazing story about resilience that started when he was a junior in high school. He had decided he wanted to be a doctor and he knew he needed more than good grades to get into medical school.

At fifteen, he went to the local hospital and asked for an application to work weekends as an orderly. He was asked what experience he had. Of course, at the tender age of fifteen, he had none. They said they weren't interested, but he could reapply in a year when he had some experience under his belt.

The very next day, Bill walked the four miles from his house to the hospital. When the secretary in the personnel office saw that he had come back, she was confused. She explained that he needed experience. He offered to complete an application, even though she said it was pointless.

The next day, Bill handed the secretary his completed application with an essay attached about why he wanted to work there. The secretary just shook her head and took the application.

Again, the next day, Bill showed up. Like a dog and a bone, he was unshakeable.

Again, he was told there weren't any openings.

He asked if he could speak with the manager for a few minutes. Miraculously, he was able to get a face-to-face meeting.

When Bill met the manager, he reviewed his goal of wanting to work there and why. The manager said no. So Bill countered with, "How about we just go over and take a walk around the operating room?"

Bill was an engaging, polite fifteen-year-old youngster, so the manager granted his wish.

During his tour of the operating room, Bill noticed a stack of surgical instruments that needed to be cleaned. He offered to start right then, cleaning those instruments, mopping the floors—anything that might need to be done.

His resilience finally paid off. The manager finally said yes.

Forty years later, Dr. Barber is a renowned breast cancer surgeon. He saves lives and gives loving care to many patients in his role as a healer.

Resilience can mean many things. It can even show up when we bounce back any time we get ignored in the hallways at work.

How many times have you passed someone in the hall—a person you have seen many times at work but don't really know—and said "Hello"?

At 6:45 a.m. on Monday mornings, in a semi-deserted

hospital hallway, I say "Hello" and get the most interesting responses from passersby.

Sometimes people smile big and share something great, even though I do not know them. They will say, "Hi! Today's my birthday!" Or, "Hey there! I leave for vacation in Florida tomorrow! Can't wait!"

I am always cheerful right back.

Other times, the person will be maybe two feet away, will look me right in the eye as I say "Hello" or "Good morning," and even though I *know* I've seen that guy at least fifteen times in the past month, he won't say a word.

No nod.

Nothing.

That happens all the dang time, I'm sad to say.

It used to bother me—until one day, when I asked my OR staff about this weird phenomenon. One of the nurses told me she gets super happy whenever this happens to her. She explained her theory of what really happens when you get the "cold-shoulder reaction" in the hallway.

She said when you get ignored like that, the universe responds with abundance and spreads all the good karma it can find, like butter on warm toast, all around you.

Several other folks in the OR nodded their heads. They had heard that story, too.

Fascinating, huh?

One nurse shared that she had even won the lottery on the same day someone ignored her cheerful greeting.

"Wait a minute. You won the lottery and you're still working here?" I asked.

"Well, it wasn't *that* much—just twenty thousand dollars," she said.

I cannot make this up.

Over the past several weeks, I've adopted a new way of interpreting people's cold-shoulder reactions to my greetings. And you know what? Things have changed.

When I say "Hello" or "Good morning" and I get nada, nothing, not even a blink, I think, "Woo-hoo! What great thing is going to happen today because of that person? Yippee!"

I am on the lookout for it all day.

And guess what?

It always happens that the universe throws me a blessing.

Case in point: Recently, I got perhaps one of the biggest cold-shoulder reactions possible. I had just parked in the doctors' parking deck and was running to catch the elevator. Another doctor was about three feet ahead of me and had entered the elevator.

The elevator doors closed when I was about ten inches from them.

Huh?

I know he saw me. He was in a hurry, too, I'm sure.

But seriously?

My first thoughts were not printable. For about twenty seconds. Then I thought, "Whoa! This is gonna be a really great karma day."

Here's how it played out: I took the next elevator and ended up passing that same doctor in the hallway. I came close to thanking him for my great karma day but decided against it. I entered the OR. My first case was running a few minutes late. Thinking my karma thing was not happening after all, I asked why we were delayed. It turned out that the nurse had noticed the patient's bed was malfunctioning, so she took the time and energy to change it out before I arrived. Yes! And all four cases I had that day went so smoothly that I was running an hour (unbelievable!) ahead of schedule.

The rest of the day was one good thing after another: Parking spot at the office? Score! Light traffic on the way home? You bet! Happy husband at the dinner table? Yes, ma'am!

So before you get your boxers in a bunch at a dismissive response to your friendly greetings, remember that the resilience that keeps you trying every day is serving you well. Because resilience can show up in all sorts of ways.

The important thing is that it does show up. Loud and clear. Every day.

**Prescriptions to Develop Resilience**

Is there a way to develop more resilience? Happily, the answer is yes.

- One way to improve your resilience is to work on your self-awareness. Become aware of your own expectations and behaviors and notice others' expectations as well.
- Reflect on the good parts of your day and pay attention to what negative factors can teach you for the future.
- Gain a modicum of control over your day. It doesn't have to be a big change. Consider the route you take to the hospital or what you pack for lunch.
- Schedule a ten-minute breather, during which you literally take a few deep breaths and regroup.
- Let your friends and family into your world by relating events during your day to help broaden your perspective.[4]

"When we learn how to become resilient, we learn how to embrace the beautifully broad spectrum of the human experience."

—Jaeda DeWalt

# CHAPTER 3

## PRACTICE
## FAITH

"Faith is a knowledge within the
heart, beyond the reach of proof."
—Khalil Gibran

**W**hen we talk about faith, people can get a little prickly. Do I mean Christian faith? Jewish faith? Mormon faith?

No, I'm talking about front-and-center faith. The kind we doctors have when we make that first incision and trust we will be able to later close the wound.

The kind of faith we rely on when we prescribe medicine to help what ails the patient.

The faith we have when we trust that the pathology report—whether good or bad—is accurate.

Faith can be defined as believing in and having complete confidence in something or someone.

As doctors, our faith started in our training. When we were in the cadaver lab for the first time, we had faith that we were examining those donated bodies for a reason. We had faith that our professors knew that the pharmacology information they made us memorize was correct. We had faith that we could live on only four hours of sleep a night and a diet of leftover pizza and coffee.

Those days, having faith was easy.

Nowadays, faith seems to be harder to come by.

Do you still have faith that you are in the right profession? Do you question whether the calling you felt years ago was real?

Do you still have faith that you can continue to treat your patients with dignity, in spite of insurance intervention, government demands, and pharmaceutical company quirks?

I believe it's time we have a little faith again.

"When doctors are dispirited, the care they give to patients is worse," said Dr. Farr Curlin, who served as founding codirector of the Program on Medicine and Religion at the University of Chicago from 2008 to 2013. Curlin and his colleagues have completed a series of national studies that review religion-associated variations in US physicians' attitudes and practices.[1]

In the past, and perhaps in some places still today, medical students and residents have been reprimanded for "showing" their faith with the cross they wore on their lapel or the need to recite prayers throughout the day.[2]

There have been many studies on the effect of spirituality and faith on patients' health; however, the impact of doctors' faith on patient health is not so clear.

I had the opportunity to interview many doctors about their perspectives on medicine and faith came up often. In talking with Dr. Chester Rollins, an otolaryngologist in one of the premier groups in Atlanta, Georgia, about how he decided to go into medicine, he recalled the concept of it being a true calling.

"If you're being pulled to do something that is your backhand, not your forehand—but you keep getting nudged towards it—then you know it is what you were made to do. The rest is easy," Rollins said.

He described the "calling" piece like a lens that brought everything into focus for him and marveled at how patients with devastating neoplastic disease would not allow themselves to be "painted into a box of conditioned hopelessness." In this way, "The patients become our teachers, rather than the other way around," he said.

Dr. Rollins described a time about fifteen years ago when he was "going through a wasteland" and felt very discouraged. A fellow surgeon reached out to him with these words of wisdom: "This is what we do. Not everybody can do it. Not everybody would want to do it. But this is what we do."

Dr. Rollins said he realized we all encounter some deserts along the way to reach those extraordinary patients; this turned it around for him. By relying on faith and finding inspiration in his patients, Dr. Rollins rediscovered meaning in medicine. Today, he finds joy in his practice.

As Dr. Rollins said, "Medicine at its best sees no limits." And I would add: life at its best sees no limits either.

I recently learned about a study by William Bengston and David Krinsley, published in 2000, in which they reported on the effect of holding a positive intention while "laying on of hands" with mice that had received transplanted breast cancer cells.[3]

The study found that the act of laying on of hands and setting a positive intention resulted in the mice living out their normal life spans. The study reported that even reinjecting the cancer cells into mice in remission had no effect.

Bengston and Krinsley suggested a stimulated immune response was at work.

And, of course, they called for further research.

What this information tells me is that having a positive intention and faith are key for doctors' success.

We know from experience that when a patient says, "Anesthesia always makes me sick," the patient will, in fact, become sick no matter how much we try to prevent it.

And when a patient declares, "I always bruise easily," they end up with bruises, no matter how delicately we proceed with surgery.

But what I love most about this study, and what I feel is so important to know, is this: regardless of the patient's intention, it's *our* intention and faith that matter. (I believe we can all agree that the mice in that study were not setting their intentions one way or the other.)

Several months ago, I was speaking with an anxious patient in the pre-op area, trying to find a way to reassure her. I gently touched her hand and said, "I'm setting my intention for this to go very well and for you to have a great result with easy healing."

Her eyes welled up with tears and she whispered softly, "Thank you."

Everything did go well, and later she told me that what I said meant so much to her that she shared the story of our brief conversation that morning with several of her friends.

I was surprised to find that I, too, was put at ease by the simple act of setting my intention. It helped me center myself before the surgery and to take a mental "time-out," which, for me, is even more significant than the required OR time-out during which we verify the patient's name, age, allergies, and procedure.

Ever since that day, I make it a point to share my intention with all of my patients. This simple act makes us both feel relaxed and at ease, and we all know *that* goes a long way. Shake your head if you must, but I encourage you to give it a try. (The results of the study showed that even nonbelievers had positive outcomes. Crazy, huh?)

I encourage you to set your intention for the outcomes you want. You can start small if you need to:

- Maybe you will intend that the coffee will be hot in the hospital cafeteria.
- Or that your baby will sleep through the night.
- Or maybe you'll send out an intention that your staff will get the paperwork right that day.

What do you have to lose?

As John Hiatt wrote in his 1987 song of the same name, "Have a Little Faith in Me."

I'm setting my intention for you, too.

**Prescriptions to Practice Faith**
Now, I'm not suggesting that you get religion. But I am going to encourage you to practice faith by trying the following:

- Have faith that your staff at the office really has the best intentions for your patients, even if your schedule doesn't always reflect it.
- Stop being a victim of conditioned hopelessness. Instead, be open to all the possibilities around you.
- Find just one thing to notice each day that restores your faith. It can be a flower blooming in your garden, the sun rising over the horizon, or something as simple as when you flick on the light switch, darkness recedes.

"Faith consists in believing when it is beyond the power of reason to believe."
—Voltaire

# CHAPTER 4

# CULTIVATE
# SELF-WORTH

"Do whatever it takes to convey
your essential self."
—Dr. Martha Beck

elf-worth is literally defined as a judgment of oneself.

But too often we see ourselves incorrectly. Instead of looking in the mirror and seeing the specialness we possess, we allow what we think other people think about us to enter the equation.

A doctor's self-worth can be tied up with a lot of other issues.

How well can we make a diagnosis?

How elegantly can we perform the surgery?

How happy are our patients? Our staffs? Our families?

How many articles have we had published or how many lectures have we given?

The list goes on and on, doesn't it?

For me, it's a daily, sometimes hourly, battle to separate my self-worth from how I think other people perceive me. We all want our patients (not to mention our staff and our families) to be head over heels about us all the time.

We want to feel we have made a difference, performed at our absolute best. We want to feel we've been the perfect doctor, the perfect parent, the *perfect* perfect spouse.

Therein lies the rub.

Perfection is the enemy of good.

In the OR, have you ever decided to tweak something a little bit, only to go from an "A-" outcome to a "C+," all in the name of trying to be a little more perfect?

A study by the MacArthur Foundation showed good self-worth to be a strong predictor of good health and long life.[1] So it seems likely that those who have a strong sense of self-worth would provide better health to others as well.

Those outside the medical profession are quick to say doctors have a skewed sense of increased self-worth and self-importance.

For those of us who live it daily, we know that most of the time we feel a strong sense of self is necessary, every day:

- When we enter the emergency room to see a patient, not knowing what to expect
- When we boldly begin a complicated case in the OR
- When we deliver bad news to a patient about their pathology report

Our patients expect us to be certain and secure in our approach, our knowledge, and our self-worth.

These traits are what make us good doctors.

Sure, some doctors are guilty of having an inflated sense of self. Those are the ones who are certain they are *really good doctors*. I'm sure we all know the types I'm talking about. But, for the most part, we all just put our scrub pants on one leg at a time. And we all feel like crap when things don't go well for our patients, even when we are doing our level best.

I had the good fortune to interview Dr. David Olansky, a dermatologist specializing in Mohs surgery for cancer patients. He revealed his thoughts on self-worth.

Dr. Olansky comes from a family of physicians. He said there was no pressure for him to become a doctor; it was just understood. He did have a short-lived stint as a trombone player. Seriously. But medicine won out.

"I can't imagine doing anything else. Medicine fits me to a T. That's one of the keys to happiness, when you find something where your karma and your dharma meet together: what you're supposed to do and what you are doing," he said.

Dr. Olansky shared a defining moment in his youth during our interview. As a fourth-year medical student, he went with his father to see a patient in a nursing home. The patient's husband met his dad at the door. When the man saw his dad, it was "like a ton of bricks had been lifted off of him."

Dr. Olansky said, "I realized no greater gift could have been given to that patient's husband. He felt powerless before he saw my dad. It turned out to be an easy problem. But it made me realize the power we have, and we don't even realize it," he said. "I see that every day. It's a tremendous gift to be able to help patients, physically and emotionally."

Dr. Olansky said his father taught him "to be authentic." He continued, "Be exactly who you are. The most important thing is to follow the Golden Rule. Treat other people as you would expect to be treated. Not everyone will like you, but you'll be authentic and genuine."

As I work with more and more doctors around the country, I am encouraged by what I am witnessing:

- Doctors who completely left medicine then returned later, refreshed and recharged
- Doctors who have slightly altered their original mode of practicing, discovered the parts of medicine they love most, then magnified them
- Doctors who have added and subtracted from their recipes until the unique flavor of their practice is perfect for them

My mission is to help those of you who are sitting on the edge to fall in love with medicine again.

I know you still have a tiny glimmer of hope in your hearts. You still believe there are subtle twists and changes that you can make to take the rough edges off. You believe there's still hope. You believe you can make what you once considered an awesome job tolerable and—on a good day—a great way to earn a living again.

How do I know? Because I have been where you are.

I've stood right there, looked at my practice, and found a flicker of hope still burning.

I examined my hope with a magnifying glass and it caught fire.

How? In part, I learned the lesson of the Russian dolls.

When I was little, I had a set of Russian nesting dolls. You've likely seen these before. They are officially called *matryoshka* dolls. Traditionally, the outer layer is a woman dressed in a long, shapeless peasant dress. The figures inside may be of either gender. The innermost, smallest doll is typically a baby turned from a single piece of wood.

What do these Russian dolls have to do with reigniting hope and self-worth? I believe they perfectly demonstrate how to shed what doesn't work in our lives so we can look to what's precious within.

As you open up and release the shell of what isn't working in your life, you get down to the next layer of what is better.

There's a reason that the innermost doll is a baby carved from a single piece of wood. It's what's most precious inside of all of us.

What's most valuable is not the outer, everyday surface that we all project, but rather the small, vulnerable piece of ourselves that we hide under layers.

Isn't it time we shed the traditional outer "doctor layer" and get back to our core selves? There, at the center, is where we are unique. Who we are at our center is the best we have to offer to ourselves and to our patients.

My way may not be your way. That's the whole point.

**Prescriptions to Cultivate Self-Worth**
How can you strengthen your feelings of self-worth on those hard days and remember the depth of your talents, knowledge, and wisdom?

According to Dr. David Lipschitz, you can start using several tactics to improve your own sense of self-worth:[2]

- Allow yourself to get your needs met, and look for the good in yourself.
- Congratulate yourself when things go well.
- Step back from negative self-talk.
- Recognize toxic relationships and aim to avoid them.
- Acknowledge bad habits that hold you back.
- Remember, knowing that you are the one who is limiting your own self-worth is more than half the battle.

"Never forget that once upon a time, in an unguarded moment, you recognized yourself as a friend."
—Elizabeth Gilbert

# CHAPTER 5

# PROMOTE
# CREATIVITY

"By disregarding intuition in favor
of science, or science in favor of
instincts, we limit ourselves."
—Bernie Siegel, MD

The word "creativity" isn't one most people associate with medicine. I mean, isn't it reserved for the artists and dreamers of the world?

I used to believe that, too. Then I realized that in medicine, creativity is an expression of new, exciting ideas. Creativity shows up in the development of new medicines, in new surgery modalities, and in new ways of approaching a disease.

Every day, doctors practice creativity, whether we realize it or not.

Don't believe me? What about the time you were quick on your feet and developed an on-the-spot plan when something abnormal came up during a surgery?

Or the day you restructured your afternoon clinic because of an emergency? You juggled an impossible schedule and made it work.

Or the time you came up with the perfect thing to say when you reassured an overanxious patient after she learned her diagnosis was cancer.

That's being creative.

In medical school and residency, the emphasis was always on science. Stick to the cold, hard facts. Just the facts, please. And now regurgitate those facts, please—backward.

In an article in *Academic Medicine*, Dr. Niamh Kelly argues for the importance of creativity in medicine, which allows doctors to be more collaborative and more productive.[1] Dr. Kelly's article goes on to say that while science may be central to medicine, promoting an environment of creativity can lead to better physicians and better patient care.

My view on the need for more creativity in medicine expanded when I interviewed Dr. Fred Schwartz, a renowned anesthesiologist who has appeared on CNN Headline News, NBC News, National Public Radio, and BBC News. He is an acclaimed expert in the use of music to reduce stress in premature babies.

Dr. Schwartz told me that when his wife, Marilyn, was pregnant with their first daughter, he decided to record his wife's intrauterine sounds with a synthesizer. He made several tapes in a studio and started a company called Transitions. It turns out that there is biologic variability in the intrauterine sounds that is a sign of health. He took the recordings to nurses in the neonatal ICU and suggested they conduct a study to see if the recordings improved oxygen saturation in newborns. His creative intuition was correct. The recordings did, in fact, improve oxygen levels in the newborns. That study was published in *Neonatal Network* and made headline news.

Dr. Schwartz also shared an amazing story that occurred when he was training as a resident. He had a patient who was injured and underwent emergency surgery. Her injuries were so severe that she remained in a coma after surgery. Dr. Schwartz checked on her every night after his shift, and during his visits, he'd play the flute.

Weeks went by, and he continued to play the flute during his visits with the patient. During one visit, he noticed a slight grimace on her face as he played. Several weeks later, he entered the patient's room to find her awake and telling the nurse how much she "hated the sound of that flute!"

Dr. Schwartz and I laughed as he told me this story. But his creativity in using the flute to stimulate her brain helped her find her way back, if for no other reason than to make that darn flute music stop.

What if he had played the guitar and she had loved it? She might have remained in her semi-sleeping state forever.

Creativity in cancer treatment is somewhat of a specialty for Dr. Fred Schwaibold, a practicing radiation oncologist in

Atlanta for the past twenty-five years. When Dr. Schwaibold began training, his only textbook was a two-hundred-page handout from MD Anderson Cancer Center in Houston, Texas. Back then, there was not even a residency program in radiation oncology.

Dr. Schwaibold told me about one of his earliest patients, a man who had lung cancer with metastatic disease. He treated the patient more than twenty years ago and continues to follow him. "I have a picture on my desk of his now-twelve-year-old daughter."

Over the years, Dr. Schwaibold has learned that "cancer is a spectrum and there are outliers. There are some people with tumors that, no matter what you do, you're probably never going to make a difference. And there are others who will probably always do well. And then there's the little clinical group of patients who, even in the setting of some metastatic disease, actually do reasonably well."

Dr. Schwaibold launched the first stereotactic body radiosurgery program in the state of Georgia. He described a patient he treated with this system who had metastatic cancer, Stage IV. Despite her dismal prognosis, her treatment was successful; at the time of this publication, she is an eight-year survivor.

"You could look at the book and say, 'Well, with Stage IV cancer, that patient needs only chemotherapy or hospice,'" he said. "That's not to say we should practice anecdotal medicine, but sometimes an enormous clinical experience and judgment are really what patients need from you as an oncologist."

Dr. Clinton D. McCord, a recently retired oculoplastic surgeon in Atlanta, was a pioneer in his field. He began his training in internal medicine, but his interest in ophthalmology was sparked during a research project on the electrophysiology of the eye. He measured the action potential of a layer in the retina.

This research subsequently went on to become a way to diagnose retinitis pigmentosa, an inherited, degenerative eye disease that causes severe vision impairment.

Dr. McCord likened his experience of performing difficult surgeries to war: "Every time you're in the operating room, there's something trying to stop you from putting things the way they should be. It's a personal challenge. And you're sending someone else back on their path. It's a chance to be respectful to your fellow man."

In the *New York Times* article "How Creative Is Your Doctor?" Dr. Danielle Ofri noted that although medicine is being pushed more and more toward standardization, she finds creativity to be crucial as medicine progresses into the future.[2]

Creative ideas can show up when you least expect them. It's as if they come out of nowhere, like a flash or an epiphany. When a flash happens, you know instinctually the next move to make. In those times, it might feel as if you are flying by the seat of your pants, but the truth is, you're trusting your instincts.

More than twenty years ago, when I was working on call in my residency program, a young father came in after he was badly injured in an explosion at work. The explosion caused significant injury to his hands and face, in particular to his eyes. He was first seen and treated in a tiny, remote hospital in Oregon, where he was stabilized and underwent a few emergency procedures.

In the world of ophthalmology, when an eye is so severely injured that it has no hope for useful vision, the standard of care is to surgically remove the eye. This helps prevent the possibility of sympathetic ophthalmia, where the other eye has an inflammatory reaction that can cause it to lose vision as well.

On that night, one of the young man's eyes was completely ruptured with no hope for useful vision. His other eye was damaged, too, with little hope of being saved.

Typically, in this type of injury, an eye doctor will immediately remove the most severely damaged eye.

But that night, for some unknown reason, the eye doctor in that small Oregon hospital called on his creativity and decided to sew the eye back together as best he could, even though it was clear that no vision was possible.

After that procedure, the patient was transported to the large city hospital where I was on call.

My attending and I began our four-hour case with heavy hearts. When we saw the significant damage to both of the patient's eyes, we were a bit overwhelmed with the young man's sad prognosis. I can still remember feeling helpless and grief stricken for this patient I had just met.

My attending slowly and methodically addressed the less damaged eye, which also had significant trauma; it was almost unrecognizable.

I assisted as best as I could and was grateful my attending was there to lend calm, clarity, and expertise to the surgery.

About halfway through the procedure, my attending had an idea. He, too, called on his creativity that night and decided to take tissue from the eye we knew couldn't be saved and transfer it to the eye that still had an ounce of hope. Don't ask me (or him) why he thought of this. This took place well before stem-cell transplants and such. It was just a thought that came to him in an instant, and he followed it.

My attending's flash of intuition and creativity changed the patient's life when he saved the less damaged eye that night. The patient had useful vision from it. And he sees from his eye to this day.

However, my attending did not take a lick of credit for helping this young man. Instead, he wrote a beautiful letter to the doctor at the tiny hospital who had decided not to remove the badly damaged eye before transferring the patient to us. My attending told the small-town doctor that his decision to try to mend the eye rather than remove it saved the young man's sight.

What an incredible blessing.

That day, my attending taught me that trusting your instincts and creativity is part of being a skilled doctor.

And with his letter, he also taught me that being kind and gracious is important, too.

**Prescriptions to Promote Creativity**

How can you promote creativity in your medical practice?

- Recognize and applaud yourself when you think outside the box. It happens more often than you realize. Teach yourself to spot it so you can encourage your creativity.

- Encourage colleagues to do the same. When you have been creative with a treatment or procedure, share it with others. You will not only share the knowledge so they can repeat it, but you will model for others how to venture into uncharted worlds.

- Talk with your patients about how they can add creativity to their treatment plans. Maybe they can take a pill with their dinner so it won't give them indigestion. Maybe they can make a blender drink with veggies and fruits to improve their nutrition instead of having ice cream every night. Your patients will be grateful for your flexibility, and you will be happier that they follow your treatment plans.

- Your staff has way more creative tips up their sleeves than you can imagine. Brainstorm with them on ways to improve patient flow, appointment-time congestion, or any number of things that will allow for happier employees and healthier patients.

"We have to continually be jumping off cliffs and developing our wings on the way down."

—Kurt Vonnegut

# PART III

## INTERPERSONAL PRESCRIPTIONS

# CHAPTER 6

## FOSTER SUPPORT

"This is your precious life.
Savor it."
—Lissa Rankin, MD

A patient codes and all available staff rush in to assist. A woman arrives to the emergency room with a severe, traumatic injury and a senior staff member steps forward to lead a team of young doctors.

A patient flails in pain and several hands reach out to subdue him to ease his suffering.

In the hospital environment, doctors work together to support patients. That's a noble calling, to be sure.

But what about support for doctors? I'm amazed at how infrequently the notion of support comes up in our medical training. In fact, it's only been recently that support of caregivers has come to the forefront. The need for support for caregivers started getting attention when more and more people who care for elderly or incapacitated patients boldly spoke aloud what was once considered unspeakable: they suffered through severe burnout, for years, in silence.

In the past few years, the notion of physician burnout and how to treat it has slowly emerged as a hot-button issue. In a breakthrough study published in *Archives of Internal Medicine* in 2012, researchers asked more than seven thousand doctors about their experiences with career-related burnout.[1]

The study found that the combination of low sense of accomplishment, detachment, and emotional exhaustion experienced by doctors in training is also present in doctors who have practiced from one year to several decades.

When compared to people working in other fields and adjusting for many variables, including hours worked, doctors came out on top in terms of burnout rates. In fact, doctors who work in areas such as family medicine, emergency medicine, and general internal medicine are at the greatest risk of burnout.

The bottom line is this: burnout in doctors not only affects doctors themselves; it affects the quality of treatment and care patients receive.

Slowly, administrators are recognizing the effects of burnout and are adjusting working conditions in hospitals and are changing clinic hours. They are also beginning to establish support networks for doctors and medical personnel.

But while these ideas are being evaluated and bandied about, what's a doctor in the trenches with patients to do in the meantime? I believe we start by building our own support networks. In my work with doctors at Love Medicine Again, many have expressed relief in just knowing that they are not alone in their feelings of apathy and emotional exhaustion.

The first step is recognizing and acknowledging the unique challenges we face in our jobs. Then we must be willing to talk about them with one another. "Grinning and bearing it" is not a successful coping mechanism.

Next, we must develop support systems in our work environments. This sounds easy, but in reality it can take time and be a bit tedious. The stigma around doctors asking for help lingers, unfortunately.

So what can we do to make headway immediately? Start at home. Rely on family and friends who are always in your corner and always have your back.

I asked Dr. Barber, the Atlanta-based breast cancer surgeon, about his personal support systems and how he prevents burnout. Dr. Barber regularly sees patients who are fearful of their diagnoses and are worried about their appearances and outcomes after surgery. His days are filled with long, grueling office hours seeing patients who look to him for encouragement and answers.

I asked Dr. Barber what support systems he relies on outside his practice to keep burnout and exhaustion at bay. Dr. Barber is a thoughtful, well-spoken surgeon who has been in the medical arena for more than twenty years. Before he answered, he paused and turned his chair away from me. He took several minutes to collect his thoughts. When he finally turned to face me again, I noticed his eyes were brimming with tears.

"It's my wife," he whispered. "It's Rosemary. If it weren't for Rosemary, I could not be the doctor I am today. I can't tell you the number of times I have had to cancel our dinner plans or her birthday celebration or have her go to the symphony with our neighbors because I had to run to the emergency room to see a patient," he said.

"Not once, in over twenty years, has she ever frowned or been upset. She understands completely and always encourages me to go take care of the patients. She has practically raised our two children on her own. I could have never done it without her."

Now I was the one fighting back tears.

As Dr. Barber and I continued talking, it struck me how lucky we both were to have supportive spouses.

You may feel your family members aren't always on board with what you do; they may not always understand what you give up to be fully present for your patients. I get that. But if you take a moment to reflect on the times they have encouraged you, the times they did listen, and the moments when they loved you in the background so that you could continue doing the work you're called to do, you will feel buoyed by their support.

But what do we do about building support systems in the workplace? Looking for support among your colleagues is a good place to start. Finding "like-minded" people at work is key to building a network of people you can trust.

In my interviews with doctors, this is the one refrain I heard time and time again.

Dr. William Zeckhausen encourages physicians to find a support group that has a mind-set of going forward rather than playing a game of "Ain't it awful?"[2]

Most of us can find plenty of the "Ain't it awful?" crowd without looking very hard. Instead, seek out colleagues who seem to be filled with hope and who go out of their way to uplift others.

Find people who would enjoy the maypole dance. Do you remember in grade school, every year on the first of May, doing the maypole dance with your classmates?

If you've never heard of this springtime ritual, you are in for a treat. Imagine a tall flagpole with streamers of different colors cascading from the top. Music plays as children dance around the flagpole, ribbons in hand, weaving and bobbing until a colorful maypole of ribbon magic stands in the center of the circle.

I remember looking forward to that event every year as springtime raised its head after a winter's sleep. The maypole dance was colorful and uplifting, and it filled us with hope for warmer weather, less homework, and summer vacation on the horizon.

Recently, I worked in the OR with an unfamiliar team; they were not my "usuals." Until then, I had been fortunate to work with a rotating group of core folks. But somehow, my regulars were all out on this particular day.

When I walked into the OR to greet my team, their response was less than enthusiastic. I reassured them that we would get through the day easily and that I would guide them. I tried not to take their reactions personally. (Don't we always go there?)

I realized quickly that an "Ain't it awful?" crowd surrounded me. The day was a bit of a struggle, to say the least.

When I asked them to name just one thing they liked about their jobs, only one person came forward with an answer. The other two whined about how it used to be and how it wasn't good now.

Sigh.

Working with that team, I felt as if I was the driver of a horse-drawn carriage. I constantly had to steer the horses in the proper direction. No one was interested in merrily clip-clopping along.

Fortunately, we made it through every case without incident. But by the end of the day, I felt tired and a bit sad. Then I had an epiphany: I realized that this is how so many of my colleagues feel every day.

As I changed clothes in the locker room, I wondered what message of hope I could wring out of the day. In the hallway, I saw a doctor I greatly admire walking in the opposite direction. We were in such a hurry that we almost missed each other. We reached out and shook hands and shared a few updates on our families. We talked about another special person in medicine we both know and marveled at how awesome he is with the staff and his patients. As we said our goodbyes, I called out to him that he had been the bright spot in my day. He laughed.

Talking with him reminded me of the way I felt after I danced around the maypole as a girl: uplifted, recharged, and full of hope for spring. If I hadn't allowed myself to be vulnerable and share with him my passion for helping doctors love medicine again, we never would have had that conversation. And I never would have gotten the boost I needed to go about the rest of my day.

I believe the support we need in the workplace is out there. We just have to find like-minded people who are willing to reach out with their ribbons of hope and dance along beside us.

**Prescriptions to Foster Support**
What can you do now to help build a layer of support around you?

- Ask yourself what one thing you can do this week that would be a step toward making your work world better. Who can you reach out to? Or who can you support by lending a hand?

- Enlarge your circle of support to include those you would like to emulate. Ask others for suggestions. Think of people in your medical world who seem like-minded. Suggest meeting for lunch or a cup of coffee.

- Look for positive input in the world around you. Read books by authors such as Rachel Naomi Remen, MD's *Kitchen Table Wisdom: Stories That Heal.* Share with others what you find that lifts you up.

- Look for support systems online or consider starting one of your own. That's what I did several years ago with my work at Love Medicine Again. It keeps me going forward, every day.

"Encourage, lift, and strengthen one another. For the positive energy spread to one will be felt by us all. For we are connected, one and all."

—Deborah Day

# CHAPTER 7

## EMBRACE COMPASSION

"Love and compassion are necessities, not luxuries. Without them, humanity cannot survive."
—Dalai Lama XIV

If you're like most doctors, you've had your share of training. As if all the training we received in medical school weren't enough, we also must take more than two hundred hours of continuing education every few years, which include many courses in ethics.

In my experience, the ethics courses skip over the important topics, such as empathy and compassion, topics doctors must employ every day when we deal with our staffs, our patients, and our families. Instead, the ethics courses are more concerned with arming us against the lure of pharmaceutical companies. They want to ensure we don't prescribe medications for the wrong reasons. That not only assumes we can't think for ourselves, it's out of touch with the real world doctors live in every day.

What we really need to learn is how to bring more compassion to our work.

Dr. William Branch, an internist and professor at Emory University School of Medicine in Atlanta, has conducted studies for two decades on teaching physicians compassion.[1] In research published in the journal *Academic Medicine*, Branch's research considered whether compassion could be learned. Although he felt compassion could not be taught in a single session, Dr. Branch noted that physicians going through a two-year program he designed scored higher on using compassion skills with patients.

Research shows a decline in compassion in doctors beginning as early as the third year of medical school, according to a study at the Robert Wood Johnson Medical School in 2009.[2]

Author Joseph Campbell coined the concept of "suffering with the patient."[3] Compassion, for Campbell, means wearing the other person's shoes and feeling for a moment what the patient feels as he struggles with a particular problem.

One doctor I spoke to understands Campbell's concept and

has used it for years. For Dr. Houston Payne, a high-level hand surgeon with Georgia Hand, Shoulder & Elbow, compassion is paramount. In our interview, Dr. Payne shared many stories about patients who had taught him lessons in compassion throughout his career. One patient in particular is etched in his mind. The patient had extensive hand injuries in addition to having a severe brain injury. In spite of the challenges his injuries presented, the patient's family remained compassionate and supportive throughout his treatment.

Dr. Payne learned that by witnessing compassion in others, you can't help but be influenced.

"You're continuously humbled when you do this job," he said.

Another patient he recalled had severed several fingers in a construction accident. It took more than twenty hours to complete the surgery. Luckily, the patient healed and regained full use of his fingers. Years later, the patient sent a letter to Dr. Payne, thanking him for his skill in treating his damaged hand. The letter also revealed that the patient had married and had recently had a son, whom he named Houston in honor of Dr. Payne.

After sharing that story with me, Dr. Payne sat quietly. "I was reading that note in my office and I had a hard time not breaking down," he said.

"Hand me the tissues," I said. He wasn't the only one in tears.

When I asked Dr. Payne what he would tell his twenty-nine-year-old self about how to be a better doctor, he said: "Try to be more empathetic. That is more important than anything else. Their situations are very different from mine. We all have worries, but they're different. Having some idea of a patient's situation really changes the way you treat people."

He contends that patients are there to help *us*, not the other way around.

"People will tell you what's wrong with them. You just have to listen. It may not be about ordering tests. Sometimes I figured out what was wrong with a patient because I was the only person who stopped and listened. It's not easy, but try to find ten minutes to listen to what they have to say," he said.

In my interview with Dr. Schwaibold, the radiation oncologist, he said, "It's been a very, very rewarding field because almost always you can help. You can't always cure, but you can help."

He told me about one of his toughest cases: a twenty-two-year-old woman had metastatic cancer and was twenty weeks pregnant.

Dr. Schwaibold said, "I remember sitting at the nurses' station saying, 'I don't even think I can walk in this room. I don't know what the hell I'm going to say to this person.' But we treated her and she lived until the baby was thirty-six weeks old and developed a healthy child. That was one of the most difficult things I've ever had to do. You think you're prepared for almost everything. But that was really hard."

Dr. Schwaibold went on to describe how important compassion and trust are in his everyday encounters with patients: "It's hard. Patients have to trust you. They have to feel this is normal. The patients tell me what they are most appreciative about is the explanations they get."

As Dr. Schwaibold sees it, "There are probably a lot of radiation therapists who are smarter and read more or can quote better literature. But what patients really need is to understand what their diagnosis is, what radiation will mean. You can't give them too much information."

Dr. Teresa Gilewski wrote an outstanding article about the way compassion can help with patients' treatment.[4] She stated that compassion not only helps to heal our patients, but it also helps us stay centered in our work; it reminds us of why we are there.

Extending compassion and empathy has changed the way I interact with my patients and their family members. Recently, after a long day of successful surgeries, I was finishing my fourth case. It was a Friday afternoon and we were on schedule, which made me happy.

I walked to the waiting area to find the family of the patient on whom I had just finished an elective procedure. I noticed her husband sitting in the corner. When he saw me, he stood up and walked toward me. I immediately smiled, held out my hand, and let him know everything had gone very well. His whole posture was tight and constricted. He looked at me with a deep frown on his face, despite my smile and reassurance.

"Everything went well," I said. "She lost very little blood. I'm very pleased with how everything went."

Yet he continued to grimace and barely nodded in response.

I tried to determine why he might be angry. We were not running late, so that couldn't be the reason. We were finishing at a reasonable time for him to get his wife home before rush-hour traffic began, so that wasn't the reason.

I continued to say a few words, searching his face for the answer.

He took a deep breath and tears welled up in his eyes. Then he let his breath out very slowly.

And suddenly it hit me.

Oh, how dumb of me. He wasn't angry with me. He was worried about his wife of forty-three years the whole time I had been in the OR. He could not let his guard down or relax until he had totally registered that all was well.

Duh.

It wasn't about me. Or any delay in our schedule. Or the traffic.

His reaction was about his deep love for his wife and his fear of her having surgery.

In my mind, it was a very straightforward procedure that I had done hundreds of times. To him, it was a major event.

I touched his shoulder and asked, "May I give you a hug?"

He melted into my hug, this big, burly older fellow. I hugged him hard and said softly in his ear so others in the waiting room wouldn't hear, "It's scary when our loved ones have surgery, isn't it?"

That's all he needed.

He finally nodded and a slow smile came upon his face.

He needed to know his wife was fine and her procedure was behind her.

He needed to be certain that all was well. He needed a little compassion.

Only then could he relax and hear what I had been saying.

It wasn't about me at all.

**Prescriptions to Embrace Compassion**

Adding more compassion to your practice will help you find more meaning in medicine. I encourage you to try these simple steps:

- Listen longer. Studies show the average time it takes for a doctor to interrupt a patient is less than thirty seconds. Stop. Breathe. Look directly at the patient and away from their medical record. Aim for two minutes. Just try.

- Show genuine interest and caring. If you are seeing them for a problem with their arm and you notice a large dressing on their forehead, ask about it. If they have missed the last few appointments, check in and find out why. Maybe their spouse is in the hospital or their child is gravely ill. You never know what other issues your patients are dealing with that day.

- You can't walk a mile in their shoes, but you can give them your full attention for ten minutes. Take time to develop a treatment plan and look for ways to work together toward healing. Remember, the patient is not the enemy. The problem is the enemy.

"Too often we underestimate the power of a touch, a smile, a kind word, a listening ear, an honest compliment, or the smallest act of caring, all of which have the potential to turn a life around."

—Leo Buscaglia

# CHAPTER 8

# ENCOURAGE CONNECTION

"When we know ourselves
to be connected to all others,
acting compassionately is simply
the natural thing to do."
—Rachel Naomi Remen, MD

Connection is the spark that ignites when you have a conversation in the doctors' lounge and you laugh at the same jokes, commiserate over the same wins or losses of the sports teams, or offer congratulations or condolences for the highs and lows we all experience.

Connection is the wave of heartfelt peace we all feel as a healthy, pink newborn baby is handed to her mother.

Connection is when you reach for an instrument from your scrub technician in the OR, and without an exchanged word, she hands you the very instrument you need.

Connection is noticing a look on the face of someone you care for—a loved one, a staff member, a colleague, a patient—and knowing something is very right . . . or very wrong.

Connection is the telomere in the DNA of finding meaning in medicine, the part that provides stability to the unit.

In the breakout book *Connected*, Dr. Nicholas Christakis and Dr. James Fowler discuss the importance of connection in our lives.[1] They contend that social-network perspectives can aid in public-health interventions. They reveal that our behaviors can influence our friends, our friends' friends, and our friends' friends' friends through social-network connections. In this way, human experiences and health behaviors can spread through the social networks. This can include the positive (such as happiness) and the negative (for example, obesity).

Scores of articles have been written on the doctor-patient relationship, the doctor-hospital relationship, and the doctor-pharmaceutical company relationship.

However, the most important connection has been ignored: the connections doctors make with one another. These relationships have a profound impact on doctors' lives and are, therefore, the ones that need fostering.

Dr. Rutledge Forney, a prominent dermatologist who

founded Dermatology Associates in Atlanta, Georgia, in 2004, stresses the importance of connections in her world.

In our interview, she confirmed that she has important connections with her family, her patients, and her staff. However, it's her connections with other doctors that support her the most professionally. Dr. Forney said joining medical organizations has enabled her to give and receive support from other doctors in the community. She feels her participation and leadership in local and regional groups helps her make important contributions to the world of medicine.

Joining peer groups or professional associations is one way to make connections. Another place to look for strengthened connections among doctors is online. More and more, doctors are turning to social networks, such as Twitter, Facebook, LinkedIn, and Google+.

These social-media platforms offer new ways to share breakthrough medical procedures or simply to encourage other doctors and share general-interest information with like-minded people.

Dr. Martin Lieberman, author of *Social: Why Our Brains Are Wired to Connect*, argues that in a workplace environment, positive feedback and experiences can rank, in some studies, as high as a pay increase.[2] One study found that employees were willing to give up almost thirty thousand dollars in yearly salary to be recognized with high praise at work. This finding suggests positive feedback for doctors and other medical staff could pave the way to improved job satisfaction in challenging conditions.

But who is going to offer that feedback? It has to start with us. We have to establish camaraderie and support each other. We must have each other's backs—not only in the unwritten code of not speaking disparagingly of other doctors but in the "He Ain't Heavy, He's My Brother" fashion.

Because only doctors truly know what doctors go through.

Recently, I was in the break room at the hospital scarfing

down a power bar between three-hour cases. The truth is, I was multitasking: eating, writing on a chart, and checking my email on my phone.

I had received an email from a businesswoman I have known for a few years. She wanted to know if I would like to join her for lunch the following week.

I had to laugh out loud.

The rest of the staff, who also were busy grabbing a quick bite in between patient cases, looked up. I read the email out loud.

"Lunch?" they all said.

Then we all did the combo of laughing and shaking our heads.

Doctors don't "do lunch."

Even when I am working in my office, taking a break and leaving the building for lunch is out of the question.

On less super-busy days, I have something slightly more like real food to eat than my usual power bar. And I heat up hot water for tea.

But always, as the water warms for my tea, I complete the morning's charts, fill out paperwork for surgery the next day, and answer questions from my staff on patient concerns.

So no—I don't exactly call that a true "lunch hour."

The invitation to lunch got me thinking of all the things doctors—and most medical staff—do differently. Here's a quick list I came up with in a few spare minutes between patients:

We don't always sleep through the night. Our pagers or phones are at the ready, whether we want them to be or not, for urgent or not-so-urgent calls, 24/7.

We don't try to see movies or eat nice dinners out when we are on call. Yes, it's annoying for others when our phones ring during a movie. But what's more disrupting is leaving the theater at the best part of the movie to meet someone in the emergency room.

We don't make appointments to take care of our own health. I know I am not alone when I admit that the few times I reluctantly dragged myself to a doctor's office, I was almost too sick to walk or drive there. I remember a time when my office staff demanded that I go to the doctor immediately. I literally asked if there was somewhere I could lie down as soon as I checked in at the front desk. It turned out that I had pneumonia.

Yes, doctors' lives are different.

But if you know me at all, you also know that I am going to find a silver lining to this story.

On the flip side of our differences are things doctors get to do that other people never experience.

We get to wear pajamas (some call them scrubs) and comfortable shoes to work. Not always but most of the time. Sometimes, the soft cloth of well-worn scrubs is the most comfy part of the day.

We get to hear people's stories, their fears, their innermost concerns. Our patients trust us. They value us enough to go out on a limb with their own discomfort to seek help.

We get to relieve pain, reduce fear, and reassure. Not always but, arguably, more often than most people do.

We are often the first to know. We are in the OR when the pathologist calls in to report that the lesion thought to be cancerous is benign.

We get to be the bearer of great news. We tell patients and their families the good news of the pathology report.

We get to see the miracle of life when a baby is born. We witness the joy of the parents and the incredible love rush that surrounds the entire room every time.

Yes, doctors experience the world a bit differently. And that's why we must unite in solidarity. We must encourage fellowship and connection because, let's face it, we're in this together.

**Prescriptions to Encourage Connection**

What can you do to improve the connection between your spouse, your family, your staff, your patients, and your colleagues?

- Start with the basics. When your spouse comes home from work, or your child walks in from school, or your patient presents in your office, start with a greeting, a hug, a handshake, a smile. Refrain from jumping in with, "Sorry, honey, but I wrecked the car today!" or "Did you pass your math test?" or "How is your heartburn today, Mrs. Smith?"

- Find the ties that bind and reinforce them. We all are flattered when someone remembers that we are from Texas or that our team won the Super Bowl or that today is our birthday. It's those little connections that help remind us we are all together in this world. Seek them out.

- Reach out to connect in new ways. Make a commitment to connect in a new way each month, whether it is going to journal club, supper club, or the hospital's steering committee meeting. That's how we did it when we were in junior high, remember? We would boldly show up at new events to get to know people. It's time to circle that concept again.

- Remember, it's all in the moments. It's in the moment you say "Hello" to the patient before you ask about their bursitis, in the moment you hug your spouse before you tell them about the leaky kitchen faucet, in the moment you ask your colleague about his kid in college before you ask if he can switch call coverage with you. Moments matter.

"Love is our true destiny. We do not find the meaning of life by ourselves alone— we find it with another."

—Thomas Merton

# PART IV

## GOING FORWARD

# CHAPTER 9

# WHAT'S
# NEXT?

Now that you have the prescriptions for what has worked for other doctors, my hope is that this book will aid you in your personal remedy to overcome burnout in your medical career.

Whether you decide to stay in medicine, take a break and realign yourself with your desires, or adjust your current medical world to something that is more fulfilling to you, it's important for you to know that—despite the perfection we all aim for—neither life nor medicine is perfect. And that's okay.

There's a concept called entrainment that I learned about from Dr. Schwartz, the flute-playing anesthesiologist. "Entrainment" is a word from the biomusicology world that means "the synchronization of organisms to an external rhythm, often produced by other organisms with which they interact socially."

Entrainment happens when you are at a concert and your foot automatically taps to the beat, or when fireflies flash their summertime glow in sync, or times in the OR when you are in the groove and it feels as if there is a rhythm to your work.

Sometimes when I'm in the OR, I ask the anesthesiologist to slightly turn down the volume of the patient's pulse oximeter, as I can feel my own pulse trying to keep time with the patient's rhythm.

What if entrainment becomes our new goal whenever we interact with each other or with our patients? What if we aim to be in such sync with each other that we get in the groove of community and compassion toward a better experience for all of us?

In my work with Dr. Martha Beck, best-selling author of *Finding Your Own North Star*, I've seen her almost "melt into" a client's mood, sinking down ever so slightly to match where they are.

Maybe, through empathy, we can try to match the cadence

we feel from one another and our patients. The music we would create would be a symphony.

I invite you to go forth into that imperfect world of ours with gratitude. And be brave and reach out to others in your community.

Together, we can all find meaning in medicine.

# EPILOGUE

Just days before I put the final finishing touches on the manuscript for this book, a snow and ice storm of epic proportions hit the city of Atlanta.

Winter Storm Leon, as it's now affectionately called, completely shut down the city.

Stories of woe were passed around and shared like high fives at a Braves game: kids slept at school, a baby was delivered on the interstate, and scores of people sat idly in their cars for hours. Or they took matters into their own hands and dumped their vehicles like chump change. Many cold, weary Atlantans walked home that night.

The day began as any other day. When my husband and I left our house early in the morning, we expected about an inch of snow. We shrugged and made jokes about the South's usual reaction when the "S word" is in the forecast: "Quick! Run to buy milk, bread, and eggs!"

It seems French toast is just the thing to cure what ails a person when it snows.

In my office that morning, I asked each patient I saw how the weather was. A few said they saw snowflakes but it was continuing to be a nonevent.

That afternoon, we finally heeded the warnings and decided to end clinic early.

Everything appeared normal until my 1:00 p.m. appointment failed to show up on time. At 1:15 p.m., my secretary called her to ensure she was going to make it. The patient said she was a mile from our office and it had taken her two hours to get there. Her drive was typically no longer than 15 minutes.

Uh-oh.

I was five minutes out of the parking garage when I realized my drive home wasn't going to be pretty.

Cars were moving at a snail's pace. Tensions were high, with lots of honking and people trying to cut into the lines.

I tried to listen to a book on CD but decided I better check the radio for road conditions. Every station repeated the same word over and over: "Horrible. Horrible. Horrible."

"Deep breath," I reminded myself.

After going only three-quarters of a mile in more than an hour, I began to get concerned. The temperature was lowering, the snow was continuing to fall, and the roads were getting slicker.

I was grateful I had a packet of Tic Tac in my car, but I was disappointed when I couldn't find a power bar in my purse.

As I inched along the slippery roads, I decided that singing out loud would be a way to lower my stress levels. I sang everything from "Row, Row, Row Your Boat" (don't ask me why!) to every Christmas carol I know to "Let There Be Peace on Earth and Let It Begin with Me."

As I watched cars in front of me spin out of control, I tried not to panic and sent them a silent blessing for safety.

As I got closer to home, I realized there was no way—even with lots of singing—that my car was going to make it up the hill that sits two miles from my house.

A quick, desperate text to my husband gave me the answer I didn't want to see: Get on I-285 and go down one exit. The route isn't as hilly.

I visualized myself in the Wonder Woman power pose and whispered, "I can do this!"

I tried to ignore my stomach as it turned over, and I inched my way to the interstate.

As I approached my exit a mile down—two hours later—I saw that no one was making it up the hill. The exit ramp was strewn with cars pointing in every direction. No one had made it to the top.

I sent another frantic text to my husband. He was also stuck but coming from the opposite part of town and equally frustrated. He advised me to go one more exit. It didn't seem like I had a choice.

I watched cars spin out of control and my singing got a little shakier.

Suddenly, my car was locked in a skid. It spun. I held on. My car spun out of control in the middle of the four lanes and ended up pointing west instead of north like all the other cars. "Breathe," I reminded myself.

Miraculously, my car made it through the skid unscathed.

I tried to turn my car in the right direction, but my tires could get no traction. I was going nowhere, fast.

Four cars and a tractor trailer were right there with me, spinning aimlessly and unable to right themselves on Ice Rink I-285.

Fortunately, four Good Samaritans stopped to help me. All they could manage to do was get my car to the edge of an on-ramp. They said I'd have to just wait inside my car.

"Me and the rest of Atlanta," I thought.

By the grace of God and the kindness of many strangers, helping hands stopped, pushed me to the shoulder, and suggested I drive on the shoulder if I could get traction the whole way to the next exit.

Flashers on, singing like a mad woman, I made it to the exit but faced another hill.

My tires spun out of control and two more kind strangers

pushed my car out. They advised me to pull into a parking lot and stop. I knew that was my only option. My car was not going farther.

I parked haphazardly and walked—slipping and sliding like a drunken sailor—to the nearest open place. It turned out to be my first visit to Taco Mac, a sports bar and restaurant.

As I looked around the room, I saw a very pregnant woman, a mom with a one-year-old girl, a guy from the gym next door, and two young, stranded guys from Ohio who made the bad decision to rent a Camaro that day.

We were a hodgepodge of wayward travelers, sharing updates on road conditions, giving one another support, and even holding crying babies so parents could eat and gather their wits.

The staff at Taco Mac took it all in stride.

Meanwhile, my husband was stuck in the parking lot from hell, searching for an empty soda can in his car so he could relieve himself. He was at least four hours from me.

I toyed with the idea of walking home, but I knew I wasn't dressed for a trek in eighteen-degree weather. I saw plenty of brave souls fall on their butts in the parking lot outside. No, walking wasn't a wise choice.

Fast-forward to the end of a very, very long night. At around 1:00 a.m., Bob from Taco Mac offered to try to drive me home. My husband had just left our home. He had abandoned his car and decided to walk home to grab our ski clothes. The plan was for him to walk to me, bring the clothes, and we would both walk the five miles back home.

I decided to take my chances on Bob instead.

Bob got me safely to the top of my street, where my husband met me with open arms.

When I walked in the house, I clicked my snow-covered heels three times with tears in my eyes. "There's no place like home," I said. And I meant it.

Weeks later, I recuperated from the effects of Winter Storm Leon and completed my manuscript. As I recalled the night of the storm, an interesting realization dawned on me: that night, I experienced every one of my prescriptions in real time.

Without forethought or conscious decision, I embodied the principles that I encourage you to live by. Here's what I mean:

I practiced resilience when I used my standby coping trick, singing. I sang as I inched along the ice-covered roadways. I sang when my car spun wildly out of control on the interstate. And I sang when I needed to boost my courage a notch.

I experienced my faith when I decided to take my husband's advice and proceed to the expressway to avoid the hills and again when I was forced to drive to the next exit. I had faith in myself and knew I could do what I needed to do.

I relied on my self-worth throughout the night but especially when I struck the Wonder Woman power pose in my mind's eye. I was not going to let a little ice and snow get the best of me.

I used creativity to boldly drive along the shoulder to the next exit. I ignored the negative voices in my head and figured out a way to solve the problem.

I depended on the support of so many kind strangers who extended their hands and hearts to help me. They pushed my car out of snow and offered their best advice in how I could safely get home. We were all in that situation together, and only through teamwork and trust could we overcome the challenges.

I extended compassion to other drivers who needed to cut in, switch lanes, or pull to the side of the road when they had had enough. I experienced compassion when I finally walked into the shelter of Taco Mac. The other road-weary travelers and the restaurant's staff welcomed me, fed me, and offered me instant camaraderie.

Finally, I felt true connection with every person who shared my experience. A snowstorm like Winter Storm Leon is a great equalizer. Residents of Atlanta united that night—from the family members waiting and worrying at home to the drivers stuck in their cars overnight to the emergency workers on shift to the brave souls who walked through the snow—all of us were connected. And ultimately, it was those connections that got us through the night.

I believe the prescriptions I offer you in this book are more than a remedy to help you overcome burnout and love medicine again. For me, they are steps in a recipe for how to live a joyous, abundant, successful life while healing those who need us most.

And isn't that why we chose medicine in the first place?

# Contributing Physicians

William Barber, MD
275 Collier Rd.
Suite 470
Atlanta, GA 30309

Rutledge Forney, MD
3131 Maple Dr., NE
Suite 102
Atlanta, GA 30305

Clinton D. McCord, MD
Retired

David Olansky, MD
3379 Peachtree Rd.
Suite 500
Atlanta, GA 30326

Houston Payne, MD
2061 Peachtree Rd. NE
Suite 500
Atlanta, GA 30309

Chester Rollins, MD
1720 Peachtree St.
Atlanta, GA 30309

Fred Schwaibold, DO
1800 Howell Mill Rd.
Suite LL10
Atlanta, GA 30309

Fred Schwartz, MD
1984 Peachtree Rd.
Suite 515
Atlanta, GA 30309

# Notes

## Chapter 1: Start Where You Are

1 Quote from Dr. Rachel Naomi Remen, Nov. 13, 2013, in teleclass led by Dr. Lissa Rankin, Whole Health Medicine Institute.

2 Stultz, Tara, "Would You Do It All Over Again?" *Medical Economics*, Oct. 22, 2010.

3 Crane, Mark, "Physician Frustration Grows, Income Falls—But a Ray of Hope." Medscape Business of Medicine, WebMD. April 24, 2012.

4 Sibert, Karen, "Burnout: The Perfect Storm of Physician Stress," KevinMD.com. Aug. 5, 2013.

5 Shanafelt, Tait; et al., "Burnout and Satisfaction with Work-Life Balance Among U.S. Physicians Relative to the General U.S. Population," *Archive of Internal Medicine*, 2012, Oct. 8; 172(18):1377–85.

6 Peckham, Carol, "Medscape Lifestyle Report 2013: Does Burnout Affect Lifestyle?" Medscape.com. March 28, 2013.

7 Sibert, Aug. 5, 2013.

## Chapter 2: Develop Resilience

1   McAllister, M., McKinnon, J., "The Importance of Teaching and Learning Resilience in the Health Disciplines: A Critical Review of the Literature," *Nurse Education Today*, 2009; 29:371–9.

2   Haglund, M. et al, "Resilience in the Third Year of Medical School: A Prospective Study of the Associations Between Stressful Events Occurring During Clinical Rotations and Student Well-being," *Academic Medicine*, 2009; 8:257–68.

3   Cloninger, C.R., *Feeling Good: The Science of Well-Being*, Oxford University Press, 2004.

4   Haglund, M.; et al.

## Chapter 3: Practice Faith

1   Brachear, M., "Balancing Medicine, Faith: U. of C. Researchers Study How Doctors Can Incorporate Their Own Religious Beliefs and Discuss Faith with Patients," *Chicago Tribune*. April 2, 2012.

2   Ibid.

3   Bengston, W.F., and Krinsley, D., "The Effect of the 'Laying on of Hands' on Transplanted Breast Cancer in Mice," *Journal of Scientific Exploration*, 2000, 14 (3):353–364.

## Chapter 4: Cultivate Self-Worth

1   Lipschitz, David, "Having High Self-Esteem is Essential to Good Health," Creators.com. April 26, 2012.

2   Ibid.

## Chapter 5: Promote Creativity

1 Kelly, Niamh, "What Are You Doing Creatively These Days?" *Academic Medicine*, Nov. 2012. Vol. 87 (11):1476.

2 Ofri, Danielle, "How Creative is Your Doctor?" *New York Times*, Well.blogs. March 14, 2013.

## Chapter 6: Foster Support

1 Shanafelt, Tait; et al., "Burnout and Satisfaction with Work-Life Balance Among U.S. Physicians Relative to the General U.S. Population," *Archive of Internal Medicine*, 2012; Oct. 8, 172 (18):1377–1385.

2 Zeckhausen, William, "Eight Ideas for Managing Stress and Extinguishing Burnout," *Family Practice Management*, 2002 April; 9 (4):35–38.

## Chapter 7: Embrace Compassion

1 Branch, William; et al., "A Good Clinician and a Caring Person: Longitudinal Faculty Development and the Enhancement of the Human Dimensions of Care," *Academic Medicine*, Jan. 2009, Vol. 84 (1):117–125.

2 Rosenthal, Susan; et al., "Humanism at Heart: Preserving Empathy in Third-year Medical Students," *Academic Medicine*, March 2011. Vol. 86 (3):350–358.

3 Campbell, Joseph, *The Power of Myth*, Anchor, 1988.

4 Gilewski, Teresa, "The Subtle Power of Compassion," *Journal of the American Medical Association*, Dec. 26, 2001, Vol. 286 (3):3083.

### Chapter 8: Encourage Connection

1 Christakis, Nicholas; Fowler, James, *Connected*, Back Bay Books, 2011.

2 Lieberman, Martin, *Social: Why Our Brains Are Wired to Connect*, Crown, 2013.

# About Starla Fitch, MD

Dr. Starla Fitch is a board-certified ophthalmologist who is fellowship trained in oculoplastic surgery (surgery of the eyelids, tear ducts, and periorbital region).

Dr. Fitch graduated from Southern Illinois University School of Medicine in 1987 after receiving her bachelor's degree cum laude from the University of Southwestern Louisiana and her master of science degree from Texas A&M University.

She completed her internship at Baylor College of Medicine in Houston and her ophthalmology residency at University of Washington in Seattle, where she served as chief resident her senior year. She went on to complete her oculoplastic fellowship at Eye Plastic Surgery Associates of Dallas. Throughout her career, she has received many honors, including election into the prestigious Alpha Omega Alpha Honor Medical Society.

In 1994, Dr. Fitch joined Eye Consultants of Atlanta, where she is the senior oculoplastic surgeon. Eye Consultants of Atlanta was founded more than forty years ago and is recognized as the premier ophthalmology group in the Southeast.

In addition to her surgical practice, Dr. Fitch has a passion to help doctors remember the amazing wonder of medicine. She established Love Medicine Again to help reduce burnout and remind doctors why they went into medicine in the first place.

She is married to Dr. Chris Vandewater, an oral surgeon. They have been fortunate to combine their love of travel with their desire to help others by participating in a medical mission to Africa. They enjoy special family time with many nieces and nephews, one of whom is following in Dr. Fitch's footsteps by attending Southern Illinois University School of Medicine.

Visit her website at www.lovemedicineagain.com.